This outline is the only one you will need to succeed on your upcoming ex

this literature upon completion!

I. WHAT IS A CONTRACT?

A. Definition-a promise or a set of promises for breach of which the law

Gives a remedy, or the performance of which the law in some way

recognizes as a duty.

B. Types of Contracts

1. Express or Implied

a. quasi contracts- a way to avoid unjust enrichment

EX: Bob paints Mikes shed on the belief that Mike would pay him $500 to do

so. Bob refuses to pay. A court would permit Bob to recover the value of his

services in order to prevent the unjust enrichment of Mike.

2. Bilateral or Unilateral

a.bilateral-exchange of promises (promise for a promise)

b.unilateral-exchange of an act for a promise.

1. If offeror clearly indicates that performance is the

only manner of acceptance

2. offer to the public clearly contemplating acceptance

c. most contracts are bilateral.

3. Void or Voidable and Unenforceable

a. Void- no legal effect from the beginning (cannot be enforced)

1. example-agreement to commit a crime

b. Voidable-one that a party may elect to avoid or ratify

(party may elect to enforce it)

1. example-contract by a minor

c. Unenforceable-otherwise valid but for which some defense

exists

1. example- statute of frauds

C. Creation of A Contract

1. Three Elements Needed to Create a Contract:

a. mutual assent (offer and acceptance)

b. Consideration

c. No defenses to formation II. OFFER AND ACCEPTANCE

A. Why have offer and acceptance rules?

1.   enable court to draw dividing line between preliminary negotiations

and closing of a bargain

4.Seal-some say enough, but modern cases and UCC no longer sub. for

consideration.

IV. NO DEFENSES TO FORMATION CAN EXIST

A. Defenses to Formation

1.Absence of Mutual Assent

a. Mutual Mistake- a mistake by both parties is defense if   1.

mistake concerns a basic assumption on which made

2. mistake has a material adverse effect on agreement

3. adversely affected party did not assume the risk

1. assumption of risk-when both parties know their

assumption is doubtful (conscious ignorance) mutual

mistake is not a defense

2. Mistake in value-generally not a defense, as courts

assume parties assume risk of determining value but

there are exceptions such as reliance on third party to

determine value

b. Unilateral Mistake-generally insufficient to make a contract

   voidable.

   1. Exception- if nonmistaken party knew or should have known of the mistake, it

   is voidable by mistaken party.

c. Mistake by Third Party (Intermediary, Transmission)-   generally

   will be operative as transmitted unless party receiving   it had

   reason to know of mistake.

d. Latent Ambiguity Mistakes-If ambiguous term, depends on

   awareness:

   1. neither party aware-no contract unless both parties intend

      same meaning

   2. both parties aware-no contract unless both parties intend

      same meaning

   3. one party aware-binding based on what ignorant party

   reasonably believed to be meaning of ambiguous words

   4. Ambiguity-intent taken into account

e. Misrepresentation and Fraud-

   1. valid defenses because they

      prevent mutual assent.

2. Must go to a material factor in the contract. 3. If fraudulent mis.-actual reliance

If innocent mis.-must be reasonable reliance

4. Fraud where party tricked into assenting without understanding the significance of her action-no contract

5. Fraud as to underlying transaction-contract voidable by frauded party

2. Absence of Consideration-lacks bargaining or legal detriment, no contract exists

3. Public Policy Defenses-Illegality of Contract

a.If consideration or subject matter of contract is illegal, contract is void.

1.Example-contract to commit a murder.

2. Exceptions

a. Π is unaware and Δ knows

b. Parties not in pari delicto (one party not as at fault as other)

c. illegality is failure to obtance license for revenue

raising purposes rather than for protection

of public

b. If purpose behind contract is illegal, contract is

voidable by party who was unaware of purpose or aware but did

not faiciliate purpose and does not involve serious moral turpitude

(like murder)

B. Defenses based on Lack of Capacity

1. Under age 18-voidable by minor but not by adult

2. Insane Persons-when insane, voidable, if lucid, then has

capacity

3. Intoxicated Persons if other party knows of intoxication

4. Duress and Coercion

C. Defenses to Enforcement

1. Statute of Frauds-must be in writing

a.executors or administrators to pay debts out of own funds

b. answer for debt or default of another

c. marriage

d. land

e. cannot be performed within one year

f. sale of goods for 500 dollars or more

g. Requirements of Statute-identity of parties, subject matter, terms and

conditions, consideration recited and signature of party to be charged

or his agent

h. Several pieces of writing btn parties sufficient

i. Only party to be charged (sued) must sign.

j. Noncompliance renders it unenforceable.

2. Unconscionability-Voidable if clauses are so one sided as to be

unconscionable. (risk shifting provisions and contracts of adhesion)

a. tested at time contract was made not later

b. often when one party has superior bargaining power

VI. RULES OF CONTRACT CONSTRUCTION AND PAROL EVIDENCE

A. Rules of Contract Construction

1. construed as a whole according to the ordinary meaning of words.

2. If inconsisentcy between provisions written prevail over printed

3.Ambiguities construed against party preparing the contract absent evidence of intent of parties 4.Courts look to custome and

usage

5. Courts generally try to reach decision that contract is valid and

enforceable

B. Parol Evidence Rule

1. Evidence of prior or contemporaneous negotiations and agreements

that contradict, modify, or vary terms is inadmissible if written contract is

intended as the complete and final expression of the parties. A merger

clause (recital that contract is complete) strengthens presumption that

written contract final.

a. Exceptions-evidence is admissible:

1. formation defects (fraud, duress, mistake, illegal)

2.condition precedent to contract

3. intent regarding ambiguous terms

4. consideration problems

5. prior valid agreement which is incorrectly stated in

writing

6. collateral agreement if it does not contradict of vary

7.subsequent modifications

IV. INTERPRETATION AND ENFORCEMENT OF THE CONTRACT

A. Introduction

Two questions:

1. Is there a present duty to perform (absolute promise or have all conditions been met or excused?)

2. Has the duty to perform been discharged?

    a. If yes-done

    b. If no-nonperformance will be a breach of contract   B. When has a promise become absolute?

        1. Difference Between Promise and Condition

a. Promise-commitment to do or refrain from doing something

b. Condition-an event the occurrence or nonoccurance of which will   create, limit, or extinguish the duty to perform (promise modifier)   c. Interpretation of Promise or Condition

        1. Basic Test is intent of parties as judged by words, prior exchanges, custom in business (when in doubt courts prefer promises)

d.   Condition or Promise-may be promise for one party and

condition for another. (example-second parties duty to pay   is

conditioned on first party's performance). May also be both   for

same party as where a prty is under duty to reasonably ensure   that

a condition comes about (secure financing)

e.   Failure of promise-breach –vs- failure of condition-relieves other party of

obligation to perform   2. Classification of Conditions

a. Time of Occurance

1. condition precedent-condition must occur before performance is

due from other party

a. Example-agreement to pay $ if my house is sold by April 1.

b. Effect of occurance-performance due

2. condition concurrent-conditions to occur at same time

a. Example-agreement to pay $ for blackacre

b. If condition has occurred, performance of the other is due

3. Condition subsequent-condition cuts off already existing duty

a. Example-agreement to pay $ for blackacre unless zoning

is changed

b. Effect of occurance-duty to perform is excused

b. Express, Implied, and Constructive Conditions

1. Express-in contract stated clearly

2. Implied-those to be inferred from evidence of parties' intention 3. Constructive-without regard to parties intention in order to ensure parties get what they bargained for (time of performance, who performs first)

3. Have the Conditions Been Excused?

a. Excuse of Condition by Failure to Cooperate-if a party wrongfully prevents a condition from occurring will not get benefit of it

b. Excuse of Condition by Actual Breach-Actual, material breach by one party excuses other's duty of coutnerperformance (minor breach may suspend duty but not excuse it)

c. Excuse of Condition by Anticipatory Repudiation

1. must be unequivocal

2. only if executory (unperformed) duties on both sides of bilateral

3. Four alternatives for nonrepudiating party

a. treat contract as repudiated and sue immediately

b. suspend his own performance and wait until performance is due to sue

c. Treat repudiation as an offer to rescind and treat contract as discharged

d. Ignore repudiation and urge performance

4. Repudiation may be retracted until the nonrepudiating party has

accepted or detrimentally relied upon it.

d. Excuse of Condition by Prospective Inability or Unwillingness to Prfrm.

1. party might have reasonable grounds to believe the other party

will be unwilling or unable to perform when performance is

due.

2. Different from anticipatory repudiation because this only raises

doubts and is not unequivocal.

3. Conduct to show Inability or Unwillingness

a. reasonable person standard

4. Effect of Prospective Failure

a. innocent party may suspend own performance until

she gets assurances of performance. If not

coming then   may treat failure as

repudiation.

5. Retraction is possible but may not be effective if other party has

changed position in reliance on prospective failure.

e. Excuse of Condition By Substantial Performance

1. If party has almost completely performed his duties, but has

   breached in some minor way, the rule of substantial performance

   avoids forfeiture of a return performance

2. Applies to constructive conditions, usually not applied if breach

   was willful.

3. Damages Offset-Sub. performance may still require to offset damages for

   incomplete performance

4. UCC-perfect tender rule but is subject to exceptions.

f. Excuse of Condition by Divisibility of Contract

   1. If party performs one of units of divisible contract, she is entitled

      to equivalent for that unit even though she fails to perform other

      units.

   2. What is a divisible Contract?

      a. performance of each party divided into 2 or more parts

      b. number of parts due from each party same and

      c. performance of each part by one party is the agreed

         equivalent of the corresponding party by the other party.

3. Installment Contracts-UCC-contract that authorizes or requires   delivery in

separate lots is an installment contract. Can only claim   total breach if

defects are such to materially impair the entire   contract.

g. Excuse of Condition By Waiver or Estoppel

1. Estoppel Waiver-indicate that he will not insist upon the   condition, but the

waiver may be retracted at any time unless   other party detrimentally

relies upon it.

2. Election Waiver-If condition is broken, party who was to have its

benefit may either terminate his liability (exit) or

continue on contract. If he does second, he is deemed to have

waived condition.

3. condition that may be waived-if no consideration given for

waiver, it must be one that is ancillary or collateral to main

purpose of contract. Otherwise, waiver is gift and not enforceable.

4. Rights to Damamges for Failure of Condition-waiving a

condition does not waive rights to damages for other defects in

performance.

h. Excuse of Condition by Impossibility, Impracticability, or Frustration   C. Has the

Duty to Perform Been Discharged?

1. Discharge by Performance or Tender of Performance

a. duty may be discharged by complete performance or tender

of performandce assuming tendering party has ability to perform

b. discharge by condition subsequent

c.discharge by illegality

d. discharge by Impossibility, Impractiability, or Frustration

1. Impossibility-objective standard-after contract was

made, nobody could perform according to terms

a.examples-death or physical incapacity, new law

making illegal, subsequent destruction of subject

b. Exception-if services can be delegated, not dischrgd

2. Impracticability-subjective tests-party encounters extreme

and unreasonable difficulty or expense due to difficulty or

expense that was not anticipated

a. example-price increase in raw materials WILL NOT

be enough to lead to discharge b/c normal risk,

could have been anticipated

3. Frustration of Purpose

a. Supervening Event that was

b. not reasonably foreseeable at time of contract

c. which completely or almost completely destroys

the purpose of the contract and

d. purpose was understood by both parties

e. discharge by recession

a.mutual recession-both parties agree to it

b. unilateral recession-party must have adequate legal

grounds such as mistake, misrpresentation, or duress.

f.discharge by release

g.discharge by substituted contract

h.   discharge by lapse of time if party's duty is a condition to the   other's duty

  and neither performs her duty

i. discharge by operation of law-(contractual duty of performance is

merged in court judgment for breach of duty)

j. statute of limitations-makes it unenforceable

VII. BREACH OF CONTRACT

A. When does breach occur?

1.promisor under absolute duty to perform and

2. duty has not been discharged   <u>B. Material or</u>

<u>Minor Breach?</u>

1. material-if as result of breach the nonbreaching party does not   receive the

   substantial benefit of bargain.   a. non breaching party may:

               1. treat contract as an end and

2. immediate right to all remedies for breach including total

                       damages

           2.minor breach with aniticipatory repudiation is a material breach

3. Test:

   a. amount of benefit received by nonbreacher

   b. adequacy of compensation for damages to injured party

   c. extent of party performance by breacher

   d. hardship to breaching party

   e. negligent or willful behavior of breaher

   f. likelihood that breaching party will perform remainder of contract

           4. Timeliness of performance-generally failure to perform by time stated

               is not material if performance rendered within a reasonable time

a. exception-nature of contract makes timely perform. Essential

or time is of the essence is provided in contract then it is material.

C. Remedies for Breach

1. Damages (compensatory, nominal, punitive)

2. Goal is to put parties in as good a position as would have been with full

performance

a. standard measure of damages-expectation

VII. REMEDIES

The law can protect the expectation, reliance, or restitution interests or some

combination of them.

DAMAGES

A. Expectation Interest

1. Goal of contract remedies—protect expectation interest

example: UCC 1-106-"put the aggrieved party in as good a

position as if the other party had full performed, but penal

damages may not be had...."

2. Where the parties *expected* to be as the result of performance 3.Policy

Reasons-no contract police, no arrests, etc to encourage performance b/c few are willing to pay for it, balance ends and costs of alternative ways and chosen

to protect expectation and hope this gives an optimal level of performance at

an acceptable cost.

4. Duty to mitigate

a. remedies generally based on encouraging aggrieved party   to

enter a substitute contract and then award damages to make   up

any loss

b. damages

loss in value+other loss

less costs avoided

less loss avoided

b. UCC—may withhold delivery, stop delivery, resell and recover

damages, recover damages for non-acceptance

1.treats buyers as if they had covered their needs from

another seller and awards damages as increased cost of

substitute contract.

2. If unable to sell goods after reasonable effort to resell at

reasonable price, then may recover contract price.   c.

substitute contract cannot be different or inferior

examples:

1. Mclaine v. 20th century- lead role in Western

different than lead role in musical

2. de la Falaise v. GBP-had to deduct from damages   the

amount she made doing radio shows-other employment

has to be substantially similar

3.Police officer had failed to mitigate damages when

another officer got job at another city and this guy   went

to college.

4. Bus driver-similar route nearby but no merit system did

not make it inferior

d. Loss volume seller principle-

1. if you could sell an unlimited number, then no duty to

mitigate damages

examples:

a. Neri v. Retail Marine-boats

b. car dealers?

c. contractors

e.Expenses occurred in mitigating damages are recoverable

f. Incidental Damages-costs of shipping, storing, going to market, etc. and are normally added to expectation damages

g.Liquidated Damages-provision in a contract that fixes the amount of damages in the event of a breach. Enforceable if not a penalty.

    1.Enforceable if:

        a.actual damages that would result in breach must be impractical or extremely difficult to estimate

        b. Amount of damages must be a reasonable forecast

    2.UCC-enforceable if the amount fixed is reasonable in light of the anticipated or actual harm caused by the breach.

        Examples: Lake River v. Corrubundum- damages were grossly disproportionate to any probable loss

    3.Policy Considerations-

        a.against penalties-compensatory damages should be enough to deter inefficient breaches and penal damages could deter efficient breaches

b.for penalties-willing to agree to clause makes

promise more credible, adds value, parties

themselves will weigh costs and benefits, paternalist   h. Special

Contracts

a. Sale of Goods-difference btn K price and mkt price when   seller

tenders or buyer learns of breach

b.UCC-if buyer breaches, seller may withhold or stop delivery

resell goods and recover the difference or ordinary damages

for nonacceptance. If buyer has already accepted goods,

buyer may recover contract price.

c. UCC-if seller breaches, buyer may reject nonconforming

goods, cancel, cover, recover goods, specific performance,

or recover damages for nondelivery

b. Sale of Land-Difference btn Kprice and fair market value

c. Employemnt-full contract price less wages actually earned

elsewhere after breach. If breached by Ee-whatever it costs   to

replace them

d.Construction-by owner-builder gets profits plus expended

costs. By builder-cost of completion plus reasonable comp.

For delay

e. Installment payments-only partial breach if a payment not made, can get only missed payment.

i. Consequential Damages-special damages above and beyond general damages. Typically lost profits. Given if a reasonable person would have foreseen at the time of entering the contract that such damages would result from the breach

   1. Can recover only those damages that arise naturally in the usual course of things or that both parties contemplated at the time of the contract

      example: Hadley v. Baxendale-didn't tell messenger

      of crank shaft would put their business on halt,

      therefore not liable for lost profits.

   2. General Rule-consequential damages can be recovered only if at the time the contract was made, the seller had reason to forsee that the consequential damages were probable result of the breach.

   3. Policy consideration-would the party have agreed to it when faced with original possibility (true assent)

j. Punitive and Nominal Damages-generally not awarded unless

breach but no actual loss is proven then nominal

k. Liquidated Damages-vaild if damages were difficult to ascertain at

the time of contract and the amount agreed upon was a reasonable

forecast of compensatory damages. If amount is unreasonable, will

be seen as penalty and not enforced.

    1. UCC-court can consider actual damages incurred in

        determining whether a liquidated damage clause is valid

    l. Proof of Damages with Reasonable Certainty

        1.General Rule-Damages can be recovered only if the

        amount is reasonable certain of computation. (not

speculative)

            a. Lost profits

                1.Existing Business-future profits can be

                reasonably estimated from past profits

                2. New Business Rule-no lost profits because

                inherently speculative

              example: new drive in movie theater

                    Today- examine each case on own merits and

                    Could possibly compare with similar business

                    In same area

b. Trend today-not to cut off damages of uncertainty

unless uncertaintiy is fairly severe (UCC-damages

are at best approximate and must be proved with

whatever definiteness the facts permit but no more)

c. Policy considerations

1. Unfair to deny Π meaningful recovery for lack

of a sufficient track record where Π had been

prevented from establishing a record because of

Δ actions.

B. <u>Reliance Interest</u>

1.Based on aggrieved parties costs (including opportunity costs)

2.Purpose to put party in position as if the promise had not been

made (1. Reliance costs, 2. Opportunity Costs)-status quo

examples:

1. buyer orders special steel which machine will

process but seller defaults and doesn't give machine. Buyer

must pay to cancel steel contract with supplier or resell

steel at losee.

2. buyer does not seek other contracts from

other sellers, and costs them chance to find others like

Mclaine

3.If you can't get expectation, try reliance:

a. if profits are uncertain

b. no unjust enrichment

c. some reason you cant get expectation   4.Injured party can recover:

a.out of pocket expenses

b. worsening of conditions (dif in value)

c. pain and suffering beyond what was bargained for

5. If Δ can prove the contract was losing one for $\prod$ then Δ doesn't

have to pay. Contract must be shown to at least break even.

C. Restitution (Unjust Enrichment)(quasi-contract)

1. Reasonable value of a benefit gained by someone.

2. Found commonly in three situations:

a. Party gives benefit under unenforceable contract because

of some defense like SofF

b. Enforceable contract and breach but contract was losing one

for innocent party

c. no contract formed but benefit gained in precontractual stage

3.Must show

a. other party has received a benefit

b.wrong/unjust for party to have that benefit

4.Conditions-one always sues for breach of contract, not breach of

conditions.

    a. failure of condition-defense and often ends obligation to

    perform a qualified promise (other party can EXIT)

        1.Effect of failure of condition must be substantial to

        exit (discharge). If other party has substantially

        performed, can't exit but you have claim for damages

        2.If you exit, you can't recover

    b.concurrent conditions-promise on one side is same as

    condition on the other (my duty to perform is conditioned

on their tender and vice-versa)

    c.tender- if you don't want to exit, you must tender (be

ready and willing to perform) then can sue for breach

    d. If a contract calls for one performance which by its

nature takes time and another which can be done instantly

the one that takes time must be done first.

6. Examples:

    a. Colonial Dodge v. Miller-man buys car, no spare tire, didn't

        meet all conditions, was allowed to discharge)

           b.Plante v. Jacobs-built house not all specifications, no material

           failure to perform, he got contract price minus damages they

           could prove

           c. Oliver v. Cambpell-if substantial performance, no restitution

7. Measurement-

    a. fair market value of benefit (what it would have cost for

        someone else to do same thing) OR   b. increase in

    value

    D. Surrogates for Normative Choices

        1. Peevyhouse-in a coal mining lease, when lesee agrees to perform

certain remedial work on the premises concerned at the end of the lease

period (to clean up)and the contract is fully performed except for remedial work, the

measure of damages is the reasonable cost of performance of the work.

        Exception-where provision breached was incidental to main

        purpose and economic benefit is grossly disproportionate to cost

        of performance, the damages are limited to dimunition in value

        (only $300) in this case

    2.Policy considerations-

a. If cost of performance is measurable and does

not involve unreasonable economic waste, then can use it, and

decrease in value is used if it would cause unreasonable economic

waste.

b. if defect in material or construction cannot be remedied without

    expenditure disproportionate to purpose

(balance expense involved and the end to be attained) (relative

economic benefit)

c. Π could recover an unconscionable and grossly oppressive damages,

    contrarty to justice.

d. If Π allowed to recover, they would get greater benefit than

    from full performance

-vs-

e.where contractor's breach is willfull, not entitled to any doctrine

of substantial performance

f. no attempt to substantially performed, contract entered clear

and understood and unambiguous, no conditions that could not have reasonably been anticipated, taking away benefits of

contract.

E. Specific Performance

If damages inadequate, can seek specific performance

a. when damages inadequate: subject matter is rare or unique

b. Available for land and unique goods but not for services b/c of   difficulty in

supervision and signifies involuntary servitude.   c. Equitable Defenses availabe

III. CONTRACT AND CONTINUING RELATIONS

A. Spouses, Friends, Nieces, Nephews

1. Husbands and Wives

a. Balfour v. Balfour- (promise to care for wife)-held no contract

because 1.no intent to be forced into it by law 2. many promises

everyday, to allow to sue would create too much litigation 3.partys

didn't intend for them to be attended by legal consequences

b. Miller v. Miller-matters pertaining to home are not to become

matters of public concern or inquiry

1.lack of consideration

2. "Husbands and Wives who are not married"

a. Marvin v. Marvin- adults who voluntarily live together and

engage in sexual activity are as competent as any to enter

into contract

3.Bait (Promises by a family member with money to influence the lives of those without it)

   a. Hamer v. Sideway- uncle told nephew he would give money if he would refrain from smoking, drinking, gambling, swearing until he was 21. He did, uncle was keeping money until ready to care for himself, uncle died, executor refused to pay, court ruled there was consideration because he gave up legal rights for a period of time.

B. Consideration

1. Consideration-

   a. benefit received by promisor or detriment incurred by prmsee

   b. bargain approach-exchange in which each party views what   she gives as the price of what she gets

   c. Enforceable element approach-any element that will make   promise enforceable

   d. Can be an act or a promise to act if performance would be consideration

      e.exception to consideration needed is reliance.

2. Unrelied Upon Donative Promises-

a. general rule- donative promise is unenforceable b/c no

consideration.   1.exceptions

a. under seal

b. relied upon

c.moral obligation created

2. NOT writing, nominal consideration (sell car for a dollar),

conditional donative promise

3. Examples:

a.   A tells B and says, I have a gift for you, if you come

over to my house, you can have it. Not an

enforceable   promise because

coming over to house is not the   price

of the gift but a way to take possession

b.   uncle promises nephew $ if he refrains from

smoking and drinking until 21. Enforceable b/c

shows uncle was willing to pay $ for

nephew's actions

-also, could be in it for his name sake

3. Relied Upon Donative Promise

a. former rule-reliance was irrelevant, donative promise unenforc.

b. Modern rule-if a donative promise induces reliance in a manner

that promisor should reasonably expect, then it is enforceable

1. Promissory Estoppel- (substitute for consideration)

Restatement- if reasonably expect to induce action and

does induce

a. principle that promisor shold be estopped

from pleading lack of consideration when promisee

has relied on donative promise

b.enforced to the extent of the reliance

a.   Most say this is in place of consideration, some say

it is a type of consideration

4. Bargain Promises

a. general rule- a bargain constitutes consideration, therefore

a bargained for promise is enforceable.

b. Equal value not required

c. Exception-if already a preexisting legal duty to perform

(antecedent duty rule)

5.Illusory Promises

a. a statement that has the form of a promise but is not a real

promise, leaves a free way out –vs- real promise-commitment

that limits ones future options   examples: I will buy insofar

as I want to buy or I will buy but

I may terminate my obligation

b. general rule-if one party makes an illusory promise in exchange for another's

real promise, neither is bound c. Exceptions:

1.Unilateral contracts- (promise in exchange for an act)

example: A promises to pay B if he cuts down tree

A wants Bs performance, not merely promise.B

Never promises to cut down tree, but does so.

A is bound to pay even though B was never bound

2.Voidable Promises   example: contract with

minor, enforceable against   A but not against child.

3. Conditional Promises   example: If A gets

Chevy dealership, she will hire B

as sales manager

5. Alternative Promises

a.   general rule-each alternative must constitute consideration

as if bargained for alone

C. The conditional gift

       1. Kirksey v. Kirksey-no consideration by moving to her brother in laws

    2. Ricketts v. Scothern-stopped working because grandfather was going

to pay her money, her actions showed reliance upon promise, therefore

enforceable

D. Statute of Frauds

1. Certain contracts must be in writing

    a. executor/administrator

    b. answer to duty of another

    c. sale of land

    d. cannot be performed within one year from its making

    e. sale of goods in excess of certain value (UCC-500)

2. Purpose

    a. evidentiary-prevents perjury and fraud by people who might

       falsely claim that contract was made when it was not

    b. caution people, remind them they are making a commitment

    c. symbol of commitment

    d. channel behavior 3. Components of Writing:

a. identify contracting parties

b. subject matter description

c. terms and conditions of agreement

4. Effect of noncompliance with statute

a. majority- contract unenforceable but not void

1. suit cannot be brought but it is valid for other purposes

b.minority view-contract void

5. If get a benefit from contract that falls within statute, other party   can

recover for value of benefit even if you can't enforce (restitution)

E. Franchises

1. Hoffman v. Red Owl- relied on agent's statements, sued, promissory

estoppel does not require that promise sued upon be able to sustain

a cause of action under contract

IV. CONTRACTS AND SOCIAL CONTROL

A. Illegal Contracts

1. If a proposed contract is legal at time of offer but becomes illegal

before acceptance, intervening illegality theory terminates offer. If

contract made and later illegal, discharged.

2. Illegal if either consideration or object of contract is illegal

3. Illegal contract is void and courts will not intercede to aid third party

    a. severable portion may be enforced

    b. Carroll v. Beardon-sale of brothel illegal

    c. policy considerations

        1. punishment may not fit the crime, may provide

            incentive to carry out illegal contract rather than back out,

                one party may have actually planned the act, so when

            equal guilt, Δ is in better position, if not equal, courts

    sometimes adjust

4. Comparative Fault:

    a. Gates v. Rivers construction company-didn't pay illegal alien because

    claimed not allowed to make contracts.

        1. if statute imposes sanctions but doesn't declare contract

            invalid specifically, look at intent of legislature

        2. contract should be enforced in this case

            a.statute doesn't declare contracts void

            b. Π knew of violation should not be allowed to benefit

c.purpose of legislature not this

b. Karpinski v. Collins-If contract is against public policy, court can refuse to

enforce (balancing test)

<u>B. Public Policy</u>

1. Courts can refuse to enforce contracts or provisions that are against

public policy

2. Balancing Test (balance public policy against enforcment with

interest in its enforcement)   3. Covenants not to compete

a. Fullerton Lumber v. Albert Torborg-tests of necessity and

reasonableness. If necessary and reasonable, then covenants

not to compete are lawful.

<u>C. Capacity to Contract</u>

1. Mental capacity

a.   Traditional rule-lacks capacity only if mental processes so

deficient that he lacks understanding of nature, purpose, effect

b.   Restatement- if unable to act in reasonable manner and other

party has reason to know of his condition (affective test)   c.

Voidable by him but not by other party

d. still liable for restitution

2. Drunk or Drugged Persons

a.temporary incapacity-test is whether so drunk or drugged

to be unable to understand nature, purpose, effect

3. Made with Minors (infacy)

    a. voidable at minor's option, minor can enforce against adult

    b. not even liable for restitution except for value of necessaries

    c. Policy reasons-protect children from own lack of judment,

        if he were able to make binding contracts, spending power would

            not be constrained by present wealth, parents would have less

        control

    D. Duress

1. Effort to establish boundary between proper and improper advantage

    taking.

2. Threats must be wrongful/illegal (no duress if threats legal)

    a. exception- employer.employee (economic duress)

3. Duress is consent induced by physical force or threats of force or   other

    wrongful threats

    a. economic duress-threat to withhold something another party

        wants is not duress because not wrongful but it is if:

1.one party threatens or commits wrongful act that

would seriously threaten property or finances and

2. no adequate mans available to avoid or prevent

the threatened loss

4. Three concerns/reasons:

a.bargaining process is unfair

b. leverage is bad (employment at will)

c. promise is bad/unfair

5. Mitchell v. CC Sanitation   where there is such an inequaloity in

terms, sacrifices, and

rights, coercion/duress can exist (threat to lose job if didn't sign

release considered duress)

6. Wurtz v. Fleischman- deal to trade real property, duty to exercise

reasonable economic power in bargaining, breach if unreasonable

cause if victim would not have acted same without threat, damages of

restitution

7. Selmer v. Blackslee-mere stress of business conditions is not duress   if Δ

not responsible for condtions

    E. Undue Influence

1.   Unfair persuasion of a party who is under domination of person

exercising persuasion

a. example: attorney influences elderly client to sell property at

unfair price

2.   Relationships fall outside impersonal market setting (gifts and

wills) 3. Odorizzi v. Bloomfield-teacher forced to resign.- There must be a

combination of undue susceptibility in the servient person and excessive

pressure by the dominating person to make the latter's influence undue

when there is no confidential relationship between the two parties.

(narrower than Restatement)

F. Misrepresentation

1. A material misrepresentation by one party makes contract voidable.

2. Obde v. Schlemeyer-termites found, LL knew of them, misrepresented

G. Relationships of Trust and Control

1. Vokes v. Arthur Murray- a statement of party with superior knowledge

may be considered statement of fact even if normally opinion (old lady

who was vulnerable and paid for tons of dancing lessons)

H. Policy Arguments for Paternalism

1. Goal of promoting efficiency by reducing transaction costs 2.If fraud

committed but not proven, agreement will be enforced which is inefficient, could lower proof requirements but widespread give victims

inalienable entitlemnt they cannot waive and therefore cannot be

fraudulently induce to abandon, deception must be more likely and less

easily provable here than in general 1

Printed in Great Britain
by Amazon

25387940R00034